Tao Teh Ching

THE WAY AND ITS NATURE

Translated by John R. Leebrick

SUFI GEORGE BOOKS
Tucson

Copyright 1962-2008 by George Arthur Lareau. All rights reserved under International and Pan-American Copyright Conventions. No part of this work may be reproduced or transmitted in any form by any means, electronic or mechanical, including photocopying and recording, or by an information storage or retrieval system, except as may be expressly permitted by the 1976 Copyright Act or in writing by the publisher.

ISBN 1-885570-38-4

Sufi George Books: http://sgbooks.sufigeorge.net

Table of Contents

Table of Contents 3
Publisher's Introduction 5
Translator's Preface 9
Introduction... 33
The Way and Its Nature 37
Endnotes 135

Publisher's Introduction

The *Tao Teh Ching*, or The Way and Its Nature, has granted its profound truths to humanity for 2,500 years.

An enduring Chinese classic and the foundation of Taoist mysticism, it is as timely today as it has been throughout the ages, especially when compared with the new paradigm of reality emerging from modern physics.

The "tao" (pronounced "dow") is the underlying, most basic characteristic of existence, the prime mover, and seems to be the same as the wave patterns described by our new physics as the "building block" of our universe and ourselves.

Thus, the *Tao Teh Ching* is an excellent companion study for anyone interested in deepening their understanding of the nature of personal and universal reality.

The appeal of the Leebrick translation comes from his personal mastery of the mystical insights of Taoism. Although the work exists in numerous English versions, typically the profound concepts and paradoxes of Lao Tse have evaded the minds of translators using an academic approach.

As Leebrick, a native Texan, points out, "It is a tremendous help, if not a necessity, for a translator to understand what is being said. This understanding only comes from study and meditation. In short, to properly translate the *Tao Teh Ching*, one must be a Taoist."

Leebrick provides an extensive discussion to aid the seeker of truth in grasping the mysteries of the *Tao Teh Ching*. He has rendered the entire translation properly for the use of the seeker.

Recently, after somewhat anxiously not hearing anything about Jack Leebrick for 20 years, I learned of his unsolved murder. He was murdered in Austin, Texas 20 years ago, about a year after I last saw him.

This very close friend of mine showed me his translation of Lao Tse's *Tao Teh Ching* some 30 years ago. I was very impressed by it and promised to publish it. So far, I have published it three times.

I was very impressed with Jack, also. His education was in history and hardware engineering, his hobby was inventing ridiculous things like a battery-operated cockroach zapper, and his livelihood was farming weed in his upstairs apartment across the street from me.

Most importantly, his passion was the *Tao Teh Ching*. Singlehandedly, he learned to read Chinese, analyzed the existing translations and critiqued them, produced his own translation based on this analysis as well as personal knowledge of the Tao from his years of meditation and reflection, and he glowed brightly when he talked about it.

I was a young father with no money, yet I promised to publish his book. I had published a few of my own books, though doing so without money meant typing mimeograph stencils and stapling covers.

I wanted to do better for Jack. I rented an IBM electric typewriter with a book type face and set the book with that. I took the mimeographed pages with a cover to a bindery and they made a paperback edition. Needless to say, it was a short print run. The result was a minimally passable but real paperback book.

I had set up as Afterimage Book Publishers, Urbana, with my own ISBN numbers, so Jack's book got listed in Books in Print and other places. An East Coast college ordered a number of copies of the book two years running. There were occasional other sales. Today, I publish a much better-looking edition.

My psychic sense, for what it's worth, tells me that Jack was shot three times by a policeman who had a ready buyer for Jack's fresh brick of cocaine. I'm sure Jack didn't put up any resistance; he was essentially gentle. But given the nature of the crime, it seems he had to be killed.

It is really strange to feel sudden shock from something that happened 20 years ago. I try dealing with it with humor: I didn't miss much over the last 20 years after all.

But I miss Jack, still, as I have for 20 years. I'm sorry to lose him as a friend, I'm sorry to learn for sure that I have lost him, and I'm sorry for the many lives he touched who also won't have any more of him.

George Arthur Lareau (Sufi George)
Tucson, Arizona USA
August 14, 2008

Translator's Preface

During my quest to understand the nature of reality and live my life in harmony with this reality, I came in contact with an ancient book called the *Tao Teh Ching*.

This book is traditionally credited to a man named Lao Tse who lived in China 2500 years ago, and it is a classic of Chinese philosophy outlining the principles of Taoist mysticism and giving instruction for individual manifestation of these principles.

The book concerns a concept called Tao (pronounced "dow"), which translates as "way" and is proposed to be the underlying, most basic characteristic of existence, even the prime mover or precursor of existence.

Calling Tao a concept is a little incorrect because Tao is best understood to be more of a non-concept.

"The way that can be told is not the eternal way."(1) (Numbers in parentheses refer to the chapter from which quotations are taken.)

To get a feeling for this idea, it might be helpful to see most of the attributes of the Tao compiled in one place.

The "way" is indescribable, nameless, empty without being exhausted, deep, unfathomable, pure, still, invisible, inaudible, immaterial, formless, imageless, indefinable, elusive, vague, profound, obscure, silent, hidden, undifferentiated yet complete, stands alone, changeless, pervades everywhere, never acts, forever without desire, ancestor of all things, and may be regarded as the mother of the world.

The Taoist mystics believe this nameless, empty, formless quality is necessarily present before those things which can be named, and have form, can come into existence.

"All things in the world are born from existence. Existence is born from non-existence."(40)

"The nameless is the beginning of heaven and earth."(1)

"The ten thousand things use from it, none are denied."(2)

"Deep and unfathomable, the ancestor of all things.... It seems to have existed before the ancestor of heaven."(4)

"Her gateway is the root of heaven and earth."(6)

"Through it we see the beginning of all things."(21)

"It pervades everywhere and is never exhausted, it may be regarded as the mother of the world."(25)

"The way begot one. One begot two. Two begot three. Three begot all things."(42)

"The world had a beginning which may be regarded as the mother of the world."(52)

While establishing the nature of the way and its function as a precursor to existence, the *Tao Teh Ching* builds mostly on these fundamental ideas to describe the nature and behavior of the Taoist sage, and gives instruction to the individual on personally beneficial mental and physical attitudes.

Also included is instruction on proper government and a large body of general wisdom.

Perhaps any distinction between advice to the sage and guidance to the individual is artificial, but some sections mention the sage or wise man by name, so could be classified in this manner.

Basically, the sage is trying to emulate the way. He holds to emptiness and selflessness in his mind. He keeps himself in harmony and without knowledge. He takes no unnecessary action and does not strive or force his will on his surroundings. He serves others rather than himself.

"The more he uses for others, the more he has. The more he gives to others, the more he possesses."(81)

He holds to humility and lowliness.

"Humility is the root of the noble. The low is the foundation of the high. This is why kings and princes call themselves 'orphans,' 'solitary men,' and 'worthless.' Is this not because they depend on humility as root?"(39)

Men hate to be orphans, solitary men, and worthless; yet princes and kings call themselves these names. Thus, a thing sometimes grows by being diminished, and is sometimes diminished by gain."(42)

Many become uneasy when the concept of emptiness or nothingness as a frame of mind is mentioned. Perhaps the following two examples of emptiness will clarify this idea.

One example is a story of a Zen master who was serving his students tea. When he came to one student, he continued to pour tea into the student's cup though his cup was full and overflowing.

The student asked, "Master, why do you continue to pour into my cup when it is full?"

The master replied, "My friend, you must first empty your cup before I can fill it."

The master was using this demonstration to show the student that he would be unable to fill the student's cup (teach him) unless the student did first empty his cup (mind).

"Rather than filling a vessel to the brim, better to have stopped in time."(9)

Another story which might help involves a wandering monk. He was crossing a brook, and dropped his begging bowl on the rocks below. He looked down and seeing the shattered bowl, said, "That was my last guru!"

How was this begging bowl a guru to the monk? What did the bowl teach him? It taught him the value of emptiness.

"With clay a vessel is molded but its usefulness rises from the emptiness within."(11)

An empty bowl is more useful for begging than a full one. There must be emptiness before something can come in. This is a fundamental and clear concept which is a little like the western ideas that "two things cannot occupy the same space at the same time" and "nature abhors a vacuum."

So this is a productive emptiness the Taoists are speaking of; an emptiness which begets something or allows something to come in.

Just like the student with the full cup, if we keep our cup full, we will not be able to learn anything. A "know-it-all" is a poor learner.

Another concept many feel uncomfortable with is "non-action." First, "non-action" does not mean inaction. Basically, the idea is to do nothing to upset things being as they are. Let things follow their own nature.

"Do that which consists in taking no action, and order will prevail."(3)

"If one desires to take the empire and mold it as he wants, I see that he will not succeed. The empire is a sacred vessel and cannot be molded. Whoever molds it, will mar it. Whoever grasps it, will lose it."(29)

"The way never acts, yet nothing is left undone. If princes and kings could keep it, all things would be transformed of themselves."(37)

"By non-action there is nothing left undone. The empire is won by not meddling. Should you meddle, you are not sufficient to win the empire."(48)

"He who acts, harms. He who grasps, loses. Therefore, the sage does not act and therefore does not harm. He does not grasp, therefore, does not lose.... Thus, he supports the natural development of all things, but does not dare to act."(64)

When can one act?

"The worth of an action is in its timing."(8)

Much instruction is given to the individual to enable him to develop beneficial mental and physical attitudes so he may live life most successfully. These attitudes separate the Taoist sage from the unenlightened.

Perhaps the most important instruction for controlling the attitude of the mind occurs in Chapter 1, where Lao Tse tells us to give up desires if we would observe the secrets of the way.

Simply stated, if we observe things (manifestations) in terms of how they fit into our lives, then our minds will not be free to observe them as manifestations of underlying secrets.

Personal attachments to things prevent us from entering the "gateway to all mystery" mentioned in Chapter 1. This particular reference to giving up desires is not from the point of view of simply being content. It is rather direction for the mental technique which will allow one to "see" properly. (See endnote for Chapter 1.)

Chapter 16 tells us to "attain ultimate emptiness. Hold steadily to the state of peace." Lao Tse says that this "ultimate emptiness" is our real nature, and is the frame of mind to which we should return. Submission to our real nature (emptiness) is "stillness" (returning to one's destiny).

Further, Chapter 16 says that returning to one's destiny is the eternal, and knowledge of the eternal is enlightenment.

Being enlightened, "he will be in accord with the way. Being in accord with the way, he will be perpetual. Then, though the body dies, he will not perish."

An important and often repeated idea is the practice of "returning." The way and the wise man continually return to non-existence, thus renewing their ability to beget.

"Returning is how the way moves."(40)

"It returns to non-existence."(14)

"Being the valley of the world, he will be sufficient in eternal virtue and returns to the uncarved block."(28)

These are the basic instructions for directing the mind.

Also, the seeker is told to practice non-action, be content, and be a "know-nothing."

"To know that one does not know is highest. Not to know this knowledge is sickness."(71)

There are a few passages in the *Tao Teh Ching* which regard proper physical attitudes so that one can increase his chances of survival. Though the words are few and simple, they form the core of the Tai Chi exercise system, and what might be called the defensive martial arts, i.e., Judo, Kung Fu, and perhaps even boxing.

I'm distinguishing between these forms and the more aggressive forms like Karate.

First, the proper attitude for the warrior:

"He who assists the ruler of men by means of the way does not conquer the world by force of arms. This tactic is likely to recoil. Wherever armies have camped, briars and thorns grow. Great wars are always followed by famines."(30)

"Fine weapons are instruments of evil omen. They are hated by men. Therefore, those who have the way avoid them.... Weapons are instruments of evil omen, not the instruments of the gentleman.... He who delights in the slaughter of men cannot get his will in the world.... He who has killed many people should weep and mourn for them with grief and sorrow."(31)

"I have three treasures which I guard and cherish: the first is compassion.... Being compassionate, one can be courageous.... Through compassion, one wins in battle and is impregnable in defense. When heaven will save a person, it protects him with compassion."(67)

"There is no calamity greater than making light of an enemy.... Therefore, when opposing armies meet, the one that is sorry will win."(69)

"A skillful soldier is not warlike. A skillful fighter is not angry. A skillful conqueror does not give battle."(68)

When conflict cannot be avoided:

"Wage war by craftiness."(57)

"The strategists have a saying: 'I dare not advance an inch, but retreat a foot.'"(69)

"When alive, a man is tender and weak. When dead he is stiff and hard.... The stiff and hard are the comrades of death. The tender and weak are the comrades of life. Therefore, an army that is hard will not win. A tree that is hard will be cut down."(76)

Judo is the art of using the opponent's force to your advantage. Kung Fu neutralizes the opponent's attack by retreat and/or redirection of the opponent's force, and then strikes while the opponent is off balance or extended.

In boxing, the general strategy is to get the opponent coming toward you and as rigid as possible. This is done by angering the opponent with irritating blows like jabs, forcing him to lunge into a punch. The opponent is then a hard tree that is ready for the ax.

There are more important physical applications for Taoism than the martial arts. There are everyday changes and benefits which result automatically from meditating on non-contention or non-striving and non-self-asserting.

It seems that the body's physical actions begin to adopt this attitude. One finds that the body begins to be more yielding in its movements. Practicing Taoism will cause a change in one's nervous system; reflexes will improve and the body will suffer less wear and tear. One will become more respectful and protective of his body.

One's physical and mental responses, once undistracted and unencumbered by the sluggish thinking of selfishness, will work up to their capacity.

"Is it not because he is without thought of self that his self is fulfilled?"(7)

First, one begins to adopt Taoist ideas on the conscious level. Gradually, these ideas or attitudes begin to seep down to the subconscious level and Taoist behavior becomes automatic. These ideas will become so much a part of one's subconscious that he will even have Taoist responses in his dreams.

What should one expect from practicing Taoism? To be superhuman? A king among men? Once one is functioning with total efficiency it might appear that he was superhuman occasionally, but these performances are really natural.

If we can match the way, then we can be the glorious personal manifestation of the secret of existence. If we can harmonize with the basic nature of reality, then we can exercise the powers of a king.

"How should the lord of ten thousand chariots conduct himself lightly before the world? If he is light, the root is lost. If he is restless, the master is lost."(26)

Any amount of proficiency will be helpful. Even a small change in behavior can mean that difficulties will occur less frequently, be less severe when they do occur, and be more ably dealt with. Perhaps even a small change could mean the difference between success or failure, life or death.

In successfully practicing Taoism, as in any other mystical discipline, there are three steps: knowing, understanding, and execution.

First one must know the idea, then must understand. Finally, the philosophy must be executed in behavior. Though changes will begin immediately, one should not be discouraged by failures. Once the ideas are understood, success will be measured by ability to execute.

Much of the *Tao Teh Ching* is devoted to instruction for proper government. Many problems we are currently faced with were also present then, and Lao Tse addressed some of his remarks to the rulers. The ideal situation for the Taoists would be to have a Taoist ruler.

The Taoist concept of proper government is very much of a "hands off" approach. The sage ruler would strive to keep to the way and let the country follow its own nature.

"The great ruler is hesitant and uses words sparingly. When his task is accomplished and the undertaking is successful, all the people will say, 'We did this ourselves.'"(17)

To accomplish this, the ruler would maintain a very low profile and do as little as possible.

"The people are difficult to govern because those above them do too much."(75)

"Do that which consists in taking no action and order will prevail."(3)

He would be as unknown as possible and without self-display.

"The highest ruler is one whose existence is barely known by the people."(17)

He would have few desires and the society would echo his example.

"Seek to exhibit simplicity and embrace the uncarved block. Diminish selfishness and have few desires."(19)

"...the people without being commanded would be harmonious of their own accord."(32)

"If princes and kings would keep it, all things would be transformed of themselves.... Absence of desire brings stillness, and the world would be at peace of its own accord."(37)

"I practice non-action and the people are transformed of themselves. I love quietude and the people become correct of themselves. I have no desires and the people become uncarved block of themselves."(57)

There would be few laws and restrictions, and no meddling or oppression.

"The more restrictions and prohibitions there are in the world, the poorer the people.... The more laws and orders are displayed, the more thieves and robbers there are."(57)

"Do not oppress their means of livelihood."(72)

Government would be dull and ignorant rather than sharp and discerning.

"When the government is dull and ignorant, the people are happy and prosperous. When the government is sharp and knowing, the people are discontented and needy."(58)

"...to govern a state without knowledge is a blessing to the state.... It leads all things to return back; only then is great harmony reached."(65)

"He constantly tries to keep them innocent of knowledge and free from desire, and insures that the crafty never dare to act."(3)

The concept or technique of "lowliness" is mentioned in the context of governments and international relations, but it has far more general applications: it is a powerful interpersonal psychological technique.

"A great state is like the low reaches of a flowing river.... The female always overcomes the male by stillness. By stillness she becomes lowly. Therefore, a great state will win over a small state.... Thus, one, by lowering itself, wins over...it is meet that a great state should become lowly."(61)

"The reason why the rivers and seas become king of the hundred valleys is because they are skilled in being lower than they.... Therefore, the sage, desiring to be above the people, must by his words place himself below them. Desiring to lead the people, he must place his person behind them."(66)

Individuals are like "states," and the techniques recommended apply to human relations. One can be much more effective in dealing with people if the approach is respectful and not overpowering; less resistance is generated and the subject is more inclined to let his energy flow into a lower vessel.

The largest division of the *Tao Teh Ching* is devoted to what might be called general wisdom. Most of the ideas are along typically Taoist lines, but some of the philosophy is shared by most of the world's philosophies and religions.

Most of the fundamental concepts of Taoism are given without being attached to the behavior or attitudes of the wise man. Among these is the usefulness of the non-existent or empty.

"Advantage is gained from what exists, but usefulness arises from what does not exist."(11)

"The empty will be full."(22)

"Greatest fullness seems empty, yet its use is inexhaustible."(45)

The doctrine of non-action and letting things be as they are:

"The empire is a sacred vessel and cannot be molded. Who ever molds it, will mar it. Whoever grasps it, will lose it."(29)

And stillness:

"The flourishing things all return to their roots. Returning to one's roots is stillness. This is called returning to one's destiny."(16)

"Absence of desire brings stillness, and the world will be at peace of its own accord."(37)

"Purity and stillness are the world's standard."(45)

Other mystical ideas in the *Tao Teh Ching* are the interdependence or relativity of opposites (mostly limited to Chapter 2), and the usefulness of imperfection.

"Greatest perfection seems imperfect, yet its use is never impaired. Greatest fullness seems empty, yet its use is inexhaustible. Greatest straightness seems crooked. Greatest skill seems clumsy. Greatest eloquence seems stammering."(45)

"The bent will be straight. The empty will be full. The worn will be new. He who has little will receive. He who has much will be perplexed."(22)

Other ideas included are the virtues of non-contention, selflessness, and non-assertiveness, the value of being content, the superiority of softness and weakness over hardness and strength, and the importance of self over wealth.

We are also advised to avoid being controlled by our senses, and to limit our speech.

"Much speech leads inevitably to exhaustion. Better to hold fast to the center."(5)

"It is natural to use few words."(23)

"Few in the world can understand teaching without words...."(43)

"He who knows does not speak. He who speaks does not know."(56)

The motivation for this project was to obtain a consistently dependable translation of the *Tao Teh Ching*.

Although previous scholars have shed much light on Lao Tse's book, there is considerable variance among their translations. Because the serious student does not wish to ponder over passages that may not be stated correctly, it is hoped that this version is accurate and will be helpful.

Why is it so difficult to translate the *Tao Teh Ching*? The major problem is that the ideas and concepts are so profound and so unusual to Western as well as to Chinese minds.

Lao Tse said, "My words are very easy to understand and very easy to practice, yet no one in the world can understand them or practice them."(70) And he was writing to the Chinese. Some of these ideas take years for a full grasp and appreciation.

What are the other difficulties in translating the *Tao Teh Ching*? Many parts of the book are written in an unusual form: paradox. A paradox isn't even supposed to be easily understood. It is defined as a statement that is seemingly contradictory or opposed to common sense and yet is perhaps true.

Also, the *Tao Teh Ching* is written in a very abbreviated or concise style which requires expansion as it is translated into English. Lastly, our knowledge of the meaning of some of the characters may be incomplete or nonexistent.

Thus, we have profound ideas, frequently expressed in a paradoxical way, written in an extremely concise style, using some characters which are not completely understood.

So, even with the best scholarship and intentions, an uninitiated translator will be "shooting in the dark" at least some of the time.

It is a tremendous help, if not a necessity, for a translator to understand what is being said. This understanding only comes from study and meditation. In short, to properly translate the *Tao Teh Ching*, one must be a Taoist.

There are myriad examples of translation errors among the English versions of the *Tao Teh Ching*. Many of these errors show that the translator does not fully grasp the spirit of Taoism.

A good example involves the end of Chapter 15, "They who hold to the way do not desire to be full. It is through not being full that they can be old and not need renewal."

A Taoist understands the desirability of not being full. The age of a man isn't important, but his state of emptiness is important. So it is through not being full that a man can be old and not need renewal. If a man can "attain ultimate emptiness," (the next sentence after the end of Chapter 15), then he needs no renewal.

This is a good section to examine because it involves an important concept presented in a paradoxical form. In addition to being profound, it is expressed in a pleasing and powerful way.

To properly translate this section and to retain its beauty and power, the translator needs to understand and convey the importance of emptiness. The paradox should be identified (a man can be old and yet not need renewal), and correctly related to the basic idea (the importance of not being full).

Following are some examples of what other translators have done with this section. Notice what is sometimes added or changed, and how the meaning is altered, diluted, or lost.

Gia-Fu Feng and Jane English say, "Not seeking fulfillment, they are not swayed by desire to change." The paradox is not given, and the meaning is changed.

James Legge says, "It is through their not being full of themselves that they can afford to seem worn and not appear new and complete." The paradox is not forcefully translated, thus weakening the impact.

Wing-Tsit Chan says, "It is precisely because there is no overflowing that he is beyond wearing out and renewal." The sage will grow old, but he will not need renewal.

Chang Chung-yuan says, "Because he never desires to reach an extreme, he can remain in the old, yet become the new." Neither the principal thought nor the paradox is clearly given.

Ch'u Ta-Kao says, "Because he is not full, therefore when he becomes decayed he can renew." He won't renew because he won't need to.

C. Spurgeon Medhurst says, "If one is not full it is possible to be antiquated and not newly fashioned." "Not newly fashioned" is a way of saying "old," so he is saying if one is not full it is possible to be antiquated and old.

John C. H. Wu says, "But precisely because he is never full, he can always remain like a hidden sprout, and does not rush to early ripening." The "hidden sprout" and not rushing to "early ripening" are compatible to Taoist thinking, but the implication is that if one is never full then he won't grow old.

A better group:

D.T. Suzuki and Paul Carus say, "Since he is not filled, therefore he may grow old; without renewal he is complete." The punctuation separates the elements of the paradox.

Arthur Waley says, "And because they do not try to fill themselves to the brim they are like a garment that endures all wear and need never be renewed (?)" The question mark is Waley's.

D.C. Lau says, "It is because he is not full that he can be worn and yet newly made." It is interesting to note Lau's footnote for this sentence: "The present text reads, 'That he can be worn and not newly made'." The negative belongs there: "That they can be old and not need renewal."

R.B. Blakney says, "It is he who, embracing the way, is not greedy; who endures wear and tear without needing renewal." The first part of the sentence could more clearly state the idea of "not being full."

The *Tao Teh Ching* has many examples of this kind of paradoxical presentation which teach a lesson while one ponders over the paradox, the solution to the paradox being a basic tenet of Taoism.

If the statements are translated correctly, the student will be able to learn the lesson. Not appreciating the basic idea in a passage can make it difficult to recognize the paradox.

If the translator does not understand the idea, it will be difficult for him to set up the passage properly for the student. This is the value of the following translation: the entire work has been rendered properly for the use of the seeker.

The translator's method was to be as faithful to the Chinese as possible, taking care to avoid marring the intended meaning by prejudice. Only one comment is hesitantly offered to aid the reader with Chapter 1 (see endnotes).

Endnotes are used only when necessary. The student is expected to notice cross-references on his own. These are very important in studying the *Tao Teh Ching*.

The newcomer to Taoism might be cautioned to be patient in his study of the *Tao Teh Ching*. Some of the ideas may be unfamiliar or expressed in unfamiliar forms. Perhaps several sections will be understood and appreciated immediately and others will follow with observation and thought. The effort will be rewarded!

What will be the nature of these rewards? The *Tao Teh Ching* attempts to describe the "mother" of existence, and "her" characteristics and behavior. If successful, it can answer many of our questions about the beginning of existence, the nature of life, and our relationships to them.

Understanding these principles, we can harmonize with them by using the suggested techniques. If we harmonize with these principles, we will suffer less "wear and tear."

We will be able to function more efficiently in the realms of physical health and actions, mental attitudes and ability, and spiritual health. These results are promised!

Lao Tse says, "Why did the ancients so highly prize this way? Didn't they say that those who seek, get; and that sinners can escape? Therefore, it is most valued by the world."(62)

John R. Leebrick
Urbana, Illinois
June, 1980

Introduction

Historical records regarding the origins of the *Tao Teh Ching* and the life of Lao Tse are incomplete. Estimates for the date of writing of the *Tao Teh Ching* vary between the 2nd and 7th centuries B.C. The existence of a Lao Tse and his authorship of the *Tao Teh Ching* are debatable questions.

The legend is that Lao Tse was born in China in 604 B.C. in the state of Ch'u, and was an official of the archives in Chou, the capitol. Lao Tse practiced the way and its virtue. His teaching aimed at self-concealment and namelessness.

Seeing the decline of Chou, he left. As he was preparing to cross the frontier, the keeper of the pass requested that he write a book for him. Lao Tse consented and wrote a book in two parts, discussing the concepts of the way and its virtue. No one knows where he died.

The book was slightly longer than 5,000 characters, and is sometimes known as the "Book of 5,000 Characters."

Possibly the *Tao Teh Ching* was more informally compiled by those of the Taoist school of thought, attributed to a Lao Tse ("old man," "old philosopher"), and gradually became accepted in is present form.

The term "Ching" ("classic") was added later as a sign of respect. The proper way of dividing the *Tao Teh Ching* into the "two parts" mentioned in the legend is not known. The division into eighty-one "chapters" occurred in the latter half of the first millennium, and is useful for reference.

The reader may note places in the text where some of the passages seem unconnected, out of place, or repeated. The *Tao Teh Ching* was originally written on bamboo slips tied together with string and rolled up. Over time, the strings may have become rotten, mixing up some of the slips.

Perhaps this might explain these seeming irregularities, or perhaps they arose from compilation. Perhaps both. Fortunately, these curiosities do not obscure the ideas the *Tao Teh Ching* is trying to convey.

Tao is usually translated as way, path, or the way people travel. It can also mean principle, doctrine, or method. Also, it can be more metaphysically taken as ultimate reality, truth, or God.

Teh is usually translated as virtue, and has moral implications similar to the English "virtue." It can also mean the characteristics a thing has obtained, or a thing's nature; also, manifestations, potentiality, active quality, or manifestation in action.

Some translators chose to carry over the words "tao" and "teh," rather than giving English equivalents. Their thinking was that the meaning of these characters is broader than their equivalents, and that it was best to let the *Tao Teh Ching* define these concepts. This may be the best method.

However, in this text, "tao" and "teh" will be translated as "way" and "virtue," respectively, relying on the context to indicate which form of tao or teh is meant.

The title is translated as "The Way and its Nature;" "way" in the broadest possible sense; "nature" in the sense of characteristics and behavior.

The Way and Its Nature

by Lao Tse

Translated by John R. Leebrick

 1

The way that can be told is not the eternal way. The name that can be named is not the eternal name. The nameless is the beginning of heaven and earth. The named is the mother of the ten thousand things.

Therefore, give up your desires if you would observe its secrets. Keep your desires if you would observe its manifestations.

These two are the same, but diverge in name as they issue forth. Being the same, they are called profound; profound and more profound, gateway to all mystery.¹

2

When the whole world recognizes the beautiful as the beautiful, there arises the idea of the ugly. When the whole world recognizes the good as the good, there arises the idea of the bad.

For is and is not produce each other. Difficult and easy complete each other. Long and short contrast each other. High and low distinguish each other. Before and after define each other.

Therefore, the sage manages affairs without taking action, and teaches not by speech, but by accomplishment.

The ten thousand things rise from it, none are denied. It gives them life, yet exacts no gratitude. It accomplishes its task, yet lays claim to no merit. It is because it lays claim to no merit that its merit never deserts it.

3

Not to exalt men of worth will keep the people from rivalry. Not to value goods which are hard to obtain will keep them from theft. Not to display what is desirable will keep them undisturbed of mind.

Therefore, in governing the people, the sage empties their hearts, but fills their stomachs; weakens their ambitions, but strengthens their bones. He constantly tries to keep them innocent of knowledge and free from desire, and insures that the crafty never dare to act. Do that which consists in taking no action, and order will prevail.

4

The way is like the emptiness of a vessel; it is used, but never filled. Deep and unfathomable, the ancestor of all things. Blunt sharpness! Unravel tangles! Temper light! Merge with dust!

Deep, pure, and still; existing forever. I do not know whose son it is. It seems to have existed before the ancestor of heaven.

5

Heaven and earth are impartial, and treat the myriad creatures as straw dogs. The sage is impartial, and treats the people as straw dogs.²

Between heaven and earth the space is like a bellows. It is empty without being exhausted. The more it is moved, the more comes out. Much speech leads inevitably to exhaustion. Better to hold fast to the center.

6

The valley spirit never dies. It is named the mysterious female. Her gateway is the root of heaven and earth. Continuous, always existing, use will not exhaust it.

7

Heaven is eternal and the earth everlasting. The reason why heaven is eternal and the earth everlasting is that they do not exist for themselves. Hence, they are able to endure.

Therefore, the sage puts his self last and it comes first; treats it as extraneous to himself and it is preserved. Is it not because he is without thought of self that his self is fulfilled?

8

The highest goodness, like water, benefits the ten thousand things and dwells in low places men dislike. But so, is close in nature to the way.

The worth of a dwelling is in the site. The worth of a mind is in its depth. The worth of associations is in their benevolence. The worth of words is in their sincerity. The worth of government is in order. The worth of business affairs is in ability. The worth of an action is in its timing. Because it does not contend, it is free from blame.

9

Rather than filling a vessel to the brim, better to have stopped in time. Continue to hammer a sword to an edge and the sharpness cannot be preserved forever. There may be gold and jade to fill a hall, but there are none who can protect them.

To be overbearing when one has wealth and honor is to bring calamity upon oneself. To retire when the work is done, and merit and fame is acquired, is the way of heaven.

10

Can you discipline your animal soul,³ hold to the one and not be separated from it? Can you concentrate your vital breath, bringing it to the suppleness of breath in a new-born babe?⁴ Can you purify your profound vision and wash it until it is free from fault?

Can you love all your people, govern the state without taking action? Can you play the role of the female while opening and shutting heaven's gates? When your intelligence penetrates every direction, can you be without knowledge?

It produces them, and nourishes them. It produces them, yet claims no possession. It works, yet makes no claim. It is the leader, but never the lord. This is called profound virtue.

☯ 11 ☯

Thirty spokes will converge in the hub of a wheel, but the use of the cart will depend on the part of the hub that is empty space. With clay a vessel is molded, but the use of the vessel will depend on the part of the vessel that is empty space. Cry out windows and doors in the room as you build, but the use of the house will depend on the empty space in the walls.

Therefore, advantage is gained from what exists, but usefulness arises from what does not exist.

12

The five colors blind man's eyes. The five tones deafen man's ears. The five tastes spoil the palate. Racing and hunting will drive a mind mad. Goods hard to come by are hurtful to a man's actions.

Therefore, the sage is for the belly, not for the eye. Hence, he rejects the latter and seeks the former.

☯ 13 ☯

Favor and disgrace are both things to be feared. High rank is, like one's body, a source of great trouble.

What is meant by saying that favor and disgrace are both things to be feared? Favor when bestowed on a subject causes apprehension. This is what is meant by saying that favor and disgrace are both things to be feared.

What is meant by saying that high rank is, like one's body, a source of great trouble? The reason I have great trouble is because I have a body. When I no longer have a body, what trouble have I?

Therefore, he who in governing the empire regards his rank as though it were his body is the best person to be entrusted with rule. He who in governing the empire loves the empire as he loves his own body is the person to whom the empire can be entrusted.

14

We look for it, but do not see it, we name it the invisible. We listen for it, but do not hear it, we name it the inaudible. We grasp for it, but do not get hold of it, we name it the immaterial. These three cannot be analyzed and blend into one.

Above, it is not bright. Below, it is not dark. Ceaseless, it cannot be named. It returns to non-existence. It is called the form of the formless, the image of the imageless, vague and indefinable.

Meet it and you will not see its front. Follow it and you will not see its back. Lay hold of the way of old in order to master the present.

To be able to know the beginning of antiquity is called the clue to the way.

15

The masters of old were subtle, penetrating, mysterious, and too profound for men to understand.

Being beyond men's understanding, we can only try to describe their appearance: cautious, like one crossing a stream in winter; watchful, like one who fears neighbors on all sides; reserved, like a guest; elusive, like ice about to melt; simple, like an uncarved block of wood; vacant, like a valley; and murky, like troubled water.

Who can make the muddy water clear? By stillness the water will gradually become clear. Who can be quiet, and then by stirring gradually quicken the still? They who hold to the way do not desire to be full.

It is through not being full that they can be old and not need renewal.

16

Attain ultimate emptiness. Hold steadily to the state of peace. All things come into being together and I see their return. The flourishing things all return to their roots. Returning to one's roots is stillness. This is called returning to one's destiny.

Returning to one's destiny is the eternal. Knowledge of the eternal is enlightenment. Not to know the eternal is blindness that works evil and brings disaster.

From knowledge of the eternal, he will be open-minded. Being open-minded, he will be impartial. Being impartial, he will be kingly. Being kingly, he will be like heaven. Being like heaven, he will be in accord with the way. Being in accord with the way, he will be perpetual.

Then, though the body dies, he will not perish.

17

The highest ruler is one whose existence is barely known by the people. Next comes one whom they love and praise. Next comes one whom they fear. Next comes one whom they despise.

If the ruler lacks faith in the people, the people will lack faith in him. The great ruler is hesitant and uses words sparingly. When his work is accomplished and the undertaking is successful, all the people will say, "We did this ourselves!"

18

When the great way fell into disuse, there arose benevolence and morality. When wisdom and shrewdness appeared, there ensued great hypocrisy. When the six family relations[5] were no longer harmonious, we had talk of filial piety and paternal love. When the country became dark with disorder, there appeared loyal ministers.

19

Abandon sagacity and discard wisdom; the people will benefit a hundredfold. Abandon benevolence and discard righteousness; the people will return to filial piety and parental love. Abandon artful contrivances and discard scheming for profit; there would be no thieves or robbers.

These three are only ornaments and are not sufficient in themselves. Rather, seek to exhibit simplicity and embrace the uncarved block.

Diminish selfishness and have few desires.

20

Abandon learning and its vexation. For is the difference between a "yes" and a "yea"[6] comparable to the difference between good and evil? "What others fear, I too must fear"—how false, superficial, and without end.

The rejoicing of the multitude partaking of the feast of the sacrifice, or going up on the terrace in spring, leave only me unmoved, showing no sign, like a baby that has not yet smiled. Forlorn, along I drift, as though homeless.

The multitude have enough and some to spare, I alone have nothing. I have the mind of a fool, muddled and confused.

Common people are bright, only I am dim. Common people are sharp and knowing, only I am dull and ignorant. Unsettled like the sea, adrift without destination like the wind.

Other men have a purpose, but I am a stubborn, rustic boor. Alone I am and different because I value and seek my sustenance from the mother.

21

The all-embracing manifestation of the great virtue follows the way and the way alone. The thing that is called the way is elusive and vague. Vague and elusive, yet within it is form. Elusive and vague, yet within it is substance. Profound and obscure, yet within it is essence.

This essence is very real, within it is truth. From the time of old until now, its name ever remains. Through it we see the beginning of all things. How do I know that the beginning of all things is so? By this!

22

"The crooked shall be straight." The bent will be straight. The empty will be full. The worn will be new. He who has little will receive. He who has much will be perplexed.

Therefore, the sage embraces the one and becomes the model for the world. He does not display himself; therefore, he shines. He does not assert himself; therefore, he is distinguished. He does not boast of himself; therefore, he has merit. He does not take pride in himself; therefore, he endures.

Because he does not compete, no one in the world can compete with him. The ancient saying, "The crooked shall be straight,"—are these empty words? Truly, to be perfect, return to it.

23

It is natural to use few words. A whirlwind does not last a whole morning. Nor does a heavy rain last all day. Who produces them? It is heaven and earth. If even heaven and earth cannot make their phenomena last long, how much less can man?

Therefore, he who follows the way is identified with the way. He who follows virtue is identified with virtue. He who loses the way is identified with loss. He who is identified with the way is gladly received by the way. He who is identified with virtue is gladly received by virtue. He who is identified with loss is gladly received by loss.

If the ruler lacks faith in the people, the people will lack faith in him.

24

He who stands on tiptoe is unsteady. He who strides cannot walk. He who shows himself does not shine. He who asserts himself is not distinguished. He who boasts has no merit. He who is proud will not endure.

From the standpoint of the way, these things are "extra food and tumors." As all things detest them, he who possesses the way does not abide in them.

25

There is something, undifferentiated, and yet complete, which existed before heaven and earth. Silent and formless, it stands alone and does not change.

It pervades everywhere and is never exhausted; it may be regarded as the mother of the world.

I do not know its name, so I call it the way. If forced to give it a name, I call it great. Being great means to be flowing on. Flowing on means to be reaching far away. Reaching far away means to be returning.

Therefore, the way is great. Heaven is great. Earth is great. The king also is great. There are four things in the universe which are great and the king is one of them.

Man models himself after earth. Earth models itself after heaven. Heaven models itself after the way. The way models itself after its own nature.

26

The heavy is the root of the light. The still is the master of the restless.

Therefore, the sage travels all day without getting separated from his baggage wagon. Though seeing magnificent sights, he remains calm and indifferent.

How should the lord of ten thousand chariots conduct himself lightly before the world? If he is light, the root is lost. If he is restless, the master is lost.

27

A good traveler leaves no track. A good speaker makes no slip. A good reckoner needs no counting slips. A good shutter needs no bolts or bars, and yet what he has shut cannot be opened. A good binder needs no cords or knots, and yet what he has bound cannot be untied.

Therefore, the sage is always good at saving men so no man is cast out. He is always good at saving things so nothing is rejected. This is called following the light.

Therefore, the good man is the teacher of the bad man, and the bad man is the material of the good man. If the one does not respect his teacher, or if the other does not love his material, though he may be intelligent, he greatly errs. This is called the essential secret.

28

He who knows the male, yet keeps to the female, becomes the ravine of the world. Being the ravine of the world, he never deviates from eternal virtue, but returns to being childlike.

He who knows the white, yet keeps to the black, becomes the model for the world. Being the model for the world, he never deviates from eternal virtue, but returns to the infinite.

He who knows glory, yet keeps to humility, becomes the valley of the world. Being the valley of the world, he will be sufficient in eternal virtue and return to the uncarved block.

When the uncarved block is differentiated, it becomes vessels. The sage uses them, and becomes the chief. Therefore, the greatest tailor does little cutting.

29

If one desires to take the empire and mold it as he wants, I see that he will not succeed. The empire is a sacred vessel and cannot be molded. Whoever molds it, will mar it. Whoever grasps it, will lose it.

Among creatures some go ahead and some follow. Some breathe hot and some breathe cold. Some are strong and some are weak. Some rise and some fall.

Therefore, the sage avoids extremes, extravagance, and excess.

30

He who assists the ruler of men by means of the way does not conquer the world by force of arms. This tactic is likely to recoil.

Wherever armies have camped, briars and thorns grow. Great wars are always followed by famines.

One who is good, resolutely achieves his purpose, then stops. He dares not venture to press for further conquest. He achieves his purpose, but does not boast about it. He achieves his purpose, but does not brag about it. He achieves his purpose, but is not proud of it. He achieves his purpose, but only because it was necessary. He achieves his purpose, but not by force.

When things reach their prime they begin to grow old. This is contrary to the way. That which is contrary to the way will soon come to an end.

☯ 31 ☯

Fine weapons are instruments of evil omen. They are hated by men. Therefore, those who have the way avoid them.

The gentleman when at home considers the left side the place of honor, but in the time of war, the right side is the place of honor.

Weapons are instruments of evil omen, not the instruments of the gentleman. He uses them only when it cannot be avoided.

Peace and quiet are most dear to his heart. Victory is no cause for him to rejoice. To rejoice in victory is to delight in the slaughter of men. He who delights in the slaughter of men cannot get his will in the world.

On happy occasions to be on the left side is the

honored place. On occasions of mourning the right side is the honored place. The second in command of the army has his place on the left, while the commander in chief has his place on the right. This means that war is conducted like a funeral.

He who has killed many people should weep and mourn for them with grief and sorrow. The victor of a battle should be received as if he were attending a funeral ceremony.

32

The way is eternal and unnamed.

Though the uncarved block seems small, no one in the world can be its master. If kings and princes would hold on to it, all things would pay homage to them of their own accord. Heaven and earth would unite to bring down the sweet dew, and the people, without being commanded, would be harmonious of their own accord.

When the block is carved there are names. As soon as there are names, one ought to know that it is time to stop. It is only by knowing when to stop that one can avoid danger.

The relationship of the way in the world may be compared to rivulets and streams that flow to the great river and sea.

33

He who knows others is learned. He who knows himself is enlightened.

He who conquers others has strength. He who conquers himself is strong.

He who is contented is rich. He who acts with vigor has will.

He who does not lose his place will endure. He who dies but does not perish has longevity.

34

The great way is all-pervading, it can be on the left and on the right. All things depend on it for life and it denies none.

It accomplishes its work, but makes no claim. It clothes and nourishes all things, but does not claim to be lord over them.

Forever without desire, it can be called small. All things return to it, yet it is not lord over them.

Thus it may be called great. Because the sage never makes a show of being great, his greatness is achieved.

35

Hold the great form and all the world will come. It will come and receive no harm, but find rest, peace, and security.

Music and dainties will make the passing traveler stop. But the way, as it passes through the mouth, seems plain without flavor.

Look, it cannot be seen. Listen, it cannot be heard. But used, it is inexhaustible.

36

What is to be shrunk must first be expanded. What is to be weakened must first be strengthened. What is to be overthrown must first be raised up. What is to be taken must first be given.

This is called subtle light. The soft overcomes the hard and the weak overcomes the strong. Just as fish should not be taken from the deep, the sharp instruments of the state should not be shown to anyone.

37

The way never acts, yet nothing is left undone. If princes and kings could keep it, all things would be transformed of themselves. If after transformation they desired to act, I would restrain them by means of the nameless, uncarved block.

The nameless, uncarved block is absence of desire. Absence of desire brings stillness, and the world will be at peace of its own accord.

38

Superior virtue does not display virtue, therefore possesses virtue. Inferior virtue never loses the appearance of virtue, therefore has no virtue. Superior virtue does nothing, but does not need to do. Inferior virtue does, but has need to do.

Superior benevolence does, but does not need to do. Superior righteousness does, but has need to do. Superior propriety does, but when no one responds, bares arms and enforces it.

Therefore, when the way is lost, virtue appears. When virtue is lost, benevolence appears. When benevolence is lost, righteousness appears. When righteousness is lost, propriety appears.

Propriety is the thin form of loyalty and faith, and the beginning of disorder. Foreknowledge is the flower of the way and the beginning of folly.⁷

Therefore, the great man dwells in the thick and not in the superficial. He dwells in the fruit and not in the flower. Therefore, he rejects the one and takes the other.

39

From of old these things obtained the one: Heaven by obtaining the one became clear. Earth by obtaining the one became settled. Spirits by obtaining the one became charged. Valleys by obtaining the one became full.

All things by obtaining the one became alive. Princes and kings by obtaining the one became upright. All of these are the result of the one.

Without what makes it clear, heaven would rend. Without what makes it settled, the earth would fall apart. Without what makes them charged, the spirits would pass away. Without what makes them full, the valleys would be dry. Without what makes them alive, all things would perish. Without what makes them upright, the princes and kings would fall.

Therefore, humility is the root of the noble. The low is the foundation of the high. This is why kings and princes call themselves "orphans," "solitary men," and "worthless." Is this not because they depend on humility as root?

Therefore, the highest fame is no fame. Do not desire to tinkle like jade, nor rumble like rocks.

40

Returning is how the way moves. Weakness is the useful quality of the way. All things in the world are born from existence. Existence is born from non-existence.

☯ 41 ☯

When the superior scholar hears of the way, he diligently practices it. When the average scholar hears of the way, he sometimes keeps it and sometimes loses it. When the inferior scholar hears of the way, he laughs out loud. If he did not laugh, it would not be worthy of being the way.

Therefore, the sentence makers have it: The way which is bright seems to be dark. The way which goes forward seems to be going back. The way which is level seems to be rugged.

Highest virtue seems like a valley. Greatest whiteness seems sullied. Abundant virtue seems insufficient. Vigorous virtue seems indolent. Purest truth seems perverted.

The great square has no corners. The great vessel

takes long to complete. The great sound is hard to hear.

The great form has no shape. The way is hidden and nameless. Yet it is the way alone which excels in imparting and completing.

42

The way begot one. One begot two. Two begot three. Three begot all things.[8]

All things carry yin on their backs and embrace yang in their arms, and are harmonized by the blending of these immaterial breaths.

Men hate to be orphans, solitary men, and worthless; yet princes and kings call themselves these names. Thus, a thing sometimes gains by being diminished, and is sometimes diminished by gain.

What others have taught, I also teach: The violent and strong do not come to a natural death. I will make this the basis of my teaching.

43

The softest thing in the world overcomes the hardest thing in the world. That which is non-existent enters where there is no space. Hence, I know the advantage of non-action.

Few in the world can understand teaching without words, and the advantage of non-action.

44

Which is dearer, fame or self? Which is worth more, self or wealth? Which is worse, gain or loss?

Therefore, he who loves things excessively will pay the highest price. He who hoards will suffer heavy loss.

He who is contented suffers no shame. He who knows when to stop avoids danger. Thus, he will long endure.

45

Greatest perfection seems imperfect, yet its use is never impaired. Greatest fullness seems empty, yet its use is inexhaustible. Greatest straightness seems crooked. Greatest skill seems clumsy. Greatest eloquence seems stammering.

Movement overcomes cold. Stillness overcomes heat. Purity and stillness are the world's standard.

46

When the way prevails in the world, race horses are turned back to hauling dung to the fields. When the way does not prevail in the world, war horses breed on the common.

There is no sin greater than to sanction desires. There is no misfortune greater than discontentment. There is no calamity greater than greed.

Therefore, he who knows the contentment of contentment, will always be content.

47

Without going out the door, one may know the world. Without looking out the window, one may see the way of heaven. The further one goes, the less one knows.

Therefore, the sage knows without traveling; sees without looking; accomplishes without action.

48

He who pursues learning increases daily. He who pursues the way decreases daily. He decreases and further decreases until he reaches non-action.

By non-action there is nothing left undone. The empire is won not by meddling. Should you meddle, you are not sufficient to win the empire.

49

The sage has no fixed mind of his own. He makes the mind of the people his mind. He is good to those who are good. He is also good to those who are not good. For virtue is goodness.

He is faithful to those who are faithful. He is also faithful to those who are not faithful. For virtue is faithful.

The sage in the world is very apprehensive, and harmonizes his mind with the world. All the people strain their eyes and ears, and the sage treats them all as his children.

50

Going forth is life, entering is death. The companions of life are three of ten.[9] The companions of death are three of ten.[10] Those living move into the realm of death, and also are three of ten.[11]

Why is this so? Because they live life too grossly. For I have heard it said that he who knows well how to care for his life will not meet rhinoceros or tiger when travelling on land. He comes out of battle untouched by weapons. The rhinoceros finds no place to thrust his horn. The tiger, no place to fix his claws. The weapons, no place to insert their blades.

Why is this so? Because, in him, there is no realm of death.

☯ 51 ☯

The way produces them. Virtue nourishes them. Matter shapes them. Circumstances perfect them.

Therefore, the ten thousand things all revere the way and honor virtue. The way is revered and virtue honored, not by order, but always spontaneously.

Therefore, the way produces them and virtue nourishes them, grows them, nurses them, completes them, matures them, feeds them, and protects them. It produces them, yet claims no possession. It works, yet makes no claim. It is the leader, but never the lord.

This is called profound virtue.

52

The world had a beginning which may be regarded as the mother of the world. When one knows the mother, one will know the children. When one knows the children, yet keeps to the mother, then, though the body dies, he will not perish.

Close the mouth and shut the doors, and all your life you will never be exhausted. Open the mouth and meddle with affairs, and all your life you will not be safe.

To see what is small is called enlightenment. To keep to the weak is called strength. Use the light, return to enlightenment, and your body will not meet with calamity. This is called practicing the eternal.

53

If I possessed the least scrap of knowledge, I should walk on the great way, and only fear straying. The great way is very level, but people prefer bypaths.

The court is very well kept, but the fields are very weedy, and the granaries are very empty. They wear embroidered clothes, and carry sharp swords at their sides. They satiate themselves with food and drink, and have too much wealth.

This is called proclaiming robbery. Surely, this is not the way.

54

What is well planted cannot be uprooted. What is well grasped cannot slip loose. Thus, your sons and grandsons shall not cease the sacrifice to your ancestors.

Cultivate it in your person, and virtue will be genuine. Cultivate it in your family, and virtue will overflow. Cultivate it in the village, and virtue will endure. Cultivate it in the country, and virtue will be abundant. Cultivate it in the world, and virtue will be universal.

Therefore from person, see person. From family, see family. From village, see village. From country, see country. From world, see world. How do I know the world is so? By this!

55

He who possesses abundant virtue is like an infant. Wasps, scorpions, and snakes will not sting him. Fierce beasts will not seize him. Birds of prey will not strike him. His bones are weak, his sinews soft, but his grip is firm.

He does not know the union of male and female, but his organ will stir. His virility is perfect. He cries all day without becoming hoarse. His harmony is perfect.

To know harmony is the eternal. To know the eternal is enlightenment. To increase life is ominous. The mind forcing the breath is strength. When things reach their prime they begin to grow old.

This is contrary to the way. That which is contrary to the way will soon come to an end.

56

He who knows does not speak. He who speaks does not know. Close the mouth! Shut the doors! Blunt sharpness! Unravel tangles! Temper light! Merge with dust! This is called profound sameness.

Therefore, he cannot be reached by intimacy. He cannot be reached by estrangement. He cannot be reached by benefit. He cannot be reached by harm. He cannot be reached by honor. He cannot be reached by disgrace.

Therefore, he is most honored by the world.

57

Govern the state by correctness. Wage war by craftiness. Win the world by not meddling. How do I know that this is so? By this!

The more restrictions and prohibitions there are in the world, the poorer the people. The more sharp weapons the people have, the more disorder in the state. The more skills and cunning men possess, the more strange things happen. The more laws and orders are displayed, the more thieves and robbers there are.

Therefore, the sage says: I practice non-action and the people are transformed of themselves. I love quietude and the people become correct of themselves. I am not meddlesome and the people become rich of themselves. I have no desires and the people become the uncarved block of themselves.

58

When the government is dull and ignorant, the people are happy and prosperous. When the government is sharp and knowing, the people are discontented and needy. "Misery is that upon which happiness rests." "Happiness is that under which misery crouches." Who knows the end?

Does not the correct exist? The correct again becomes the perverse, and the good again becomes the evil. The people have been bewildered for a long time.

Therefore, the sage is square, but does not cut. He has corners, but does not injure. He is straightforward, but does not extend. He is bright, but does not dazzle.

59

In ruling men and serving heaven, there is nothing like frugality. It is through frugality that he is said to be returning quickly. Returning quickly means to accumulate virtue in abundance. By accumulating virtue in abundance there is nothing he cannot overcome. If there is nothing he cannot overcome, no one knows his limit. When no one knows his limit, he can possess a state.

He who possesses the mother of a state may endure long. This is called deep roots and firm stalks, the way of long life and everlasting vision.

60

Governing a great state is like cooking a small fish.[12] When the way rules the empire, evil spirits have no power, but their power doesn't harm people. Not that their power doesn't harm people, but the sage also doesn't harm people.

Since both do not harm each other, therefore their virtue will converge.

61

A great state is like the low reaches of a flowing river. It is the converging place of the world. It is the female of the world. The female always overcomes the male by stillness. By stillness she becomes lowly.

Therefore, a great state by lowering itself towards a small state will win over the small state. A small state by lowering itself towards a great state will win over the great state.

Thus, one, by lowering itself, wins over; the other is lowly, but wins over. A great state only desires to unite and nourish people. A small state only desires to be received and serve people. Since each obtains what they want, it is meet that a great state should become lowly.

62

The way is the most honored of all things: the treasure of a good man, the refuge of the bad man. Fine words can be sold for honor. Noble deeds can gain men's respect. Even if a man is bad, why should he be cast away?

Therefore, on the day the emperor is enthroned, and the three ministers appointed, rather than presenting jade disks followed by a team of horses, better to offer the way without stirring from one's seat.

Why did the ancients so highly prize this way? Didn't they say that those who seek, get; and that sinners can escape? Therefore, it is most valued by the world.

63

Act without action! Do without doing! Taste without tasting! Great, small, many, few, require injury with virtue.

Prepare for the difficult while easy. Do the great while small. Difficult things in the world had their beginnings in what was easy. Great things in the world had their beginnings in what was small.

Therefore, the sage never does the great, and thus is greatness achieved. He who makes rash promises surely keeps little faith. He who considers many things easy will meet many difficulties.

Therefore, the sage regards things as difficult and therefore never meets difficulty.

64

That which is still is easy to hold. That which has not manifested itself is easy to plan for. That which is brittle is easy to break. That which is small is easy to scatter. Act before a thing exists.

Establish order before disorder begins. The tree which fills a man's arms grows from a tiny shoot. The tower of nine stories begins with a heap of earth. A journey of a thousand miles begins with a single step.

He who acts, harms. He who grasps, loses. Therefore, the sage does not act and therefore does not harm. He does not grasp, therefore does not lose.

People in conducting their affairs, constantly harm them when they are on the verge of completion. Remain as careful at the end as at the beginning, and you will not harm affairs.

Therefore, the sage desires not to desire, and does not value things difficult to get. He learns to be unlearned and returns to what the multitudes have passed by. Thus, he supports the natural development of all things, but does not dare to act.

65

In ancient times, those who were skilled in the way did not enlighten the people, but kept them ignorant. People are difficult to govern because they have too much knowledge. To govern a state by knowledge is to rob the state. To govern a state without knowledge is a blessing to the state.

He who knows these two things has a model and standard. Always to know this model and standard is called profound virtue. Profound virtue is deep and far reaching. It leads all things to return back; only then is great harmony reached.

66

The reason why the rivers and seas become kings of the hundred valleys is because they are skilled in being lower than them. Thus, they become kings of the hundred valleys.

Therefore, the sage, desiring to be above the people, must by his words place himself below them. Desiring to lead the people, he must place his person behind them.

Therefore, the sage is above the people, but they do not feel his weight. He is ahead of the people, but they do not feel harmed. Therefore, the world rejoices in supporting him, and doesn't tire of him. Because he does not strive, no one in the world can strive with him.

67

The world says that my way is great, but resembles nothing. It is just because it is great that it resembles nothing. If it resembled anything, it would have long since been small.

I have three treasures which I guard and cherish: The first is compassion, the second is frugality, the third is not daring to be first in the world. Being compassionate, one can be courageous. Being frugal, one can be generous. Not daring to be first in the world, one can be chief of all vessels.

Nowadays, men forsake compassion to be courageous; they forsake frugality to be generous; they forsake following behind, seeking to be first. This is death.

Through compassion, one wins in battle and is impregnable in defense. When heaven will save a person, it protects him with compassion.

68

A skilful soldier is not warlike. A skillful fighter is not angry. A skillful conqueror does not give battle. A skillful employer of men is humble before them.

This is called the virtue of non-striving. This is called the ability to use men. This is called matching heaven, highest of old.

69

The strategists have a saying: I dare not act the host, but act the guest. I dare not advance an inch, but retreat a foot. This is called marching without marching; rolling up one's sleeves without baring arms; charging enemies without enemies; arming without weapons.

There is no calamity greater than to make light of an enemy. Making light of an enemy is near to losing my treasures. Therefore, when opposing armies meet, the one that is sorry will win.

70

My words are very easy to understand and very easy to practice, yet no one in the world can understand them or practice them. My words have an ancestor. My deeds have a master. It is because people do not understand this that they do not know me.

Those who know me are few, and on that account I am more honored. Therefore, the sage wears clothes of coarse cloth, but carries jade in his bosom.

71

To know that one does not know is highest. Not to know this knowledge is sickness. Only when one is sick of sickness can one not be sick.

The sage is not sick. Because he is sick of sickness, therefore he is not sick.

72

When the people do not fear what is dreadful, then a greater dread will come on them. Do not narrow their dwelling. Do not oppress their means of livelihood. Only when you do not oppress them, will they not be oppressed.

Therefore, the sage knows himself, but does not display himself. He loves himself, but does not exalt himself. Therefore, he rejects the one and takes the other.

73

He who is courageous in daring will be killed. He who is courageous in not daring will stay alive. Of these two, one is beneficial, one is harmful. Some things are loathed by heaven, who knows why?

Therefore, the sage regards things as difficult. The way of heaven does not strive, yet surely conquers. It does not speak, yet surely responds. It does not call, yet all come of themselves. It seems leisurely, yet surely plans. Heaven's net is vast, vast. The mesh is wide, yet nothing slips through.

74

When the people are not afraid of death, what use is it to frighten them with death? If the people were always afraid of death, and we could seize those who broke the law, and kill them, who would dare to?

There is always the executioner who kills. To take the place of the executioner who kills is like hewing wood for the master carpenter. He who hews wood for the master carpenter is very likely to cut his own hands.

75

The people starve because those above them eat too much taxes. Therefore, they starve. The people are difficult to govern because those above them do too much. Therefore, they are difficult to govern. The people are light of death because those above them seek after life too vigorously. Therefore, they make light of death.

Only one who is not bent on life is worthier than those who prize life.

76

When alive, a man is tender and weak. When dead, he is stiff and hard. When alive, all things, plants, and trees are tender and pliant. When dead, they are withered and dry.

Thus, the stiff and hard are the comrades of death. The tender and weak are the comrades of life.

Therefore, an army that is hard will not win. A tree that is hard will be cut down. The hard and great are below. The tender and weak are above.

☯ 77 ☯

Is not the way of heaven like the bending of a bow? The high it brings down. The low it raises up. Those who have too much it takes from. Those who are deficient it supplements.

The way of heaven takes from those who have too much and supplements those who are deficient. The way of man is not so. He takes from those who are deficient to give to those who have too much. Who can take his too much and give to the world? Only he who has the way.

Therefore, the sage works, yet makes no claim. Accomplishes his task, yet claims no merit. He does not desire to display his superiority.

78

Nothing in the world is more soft and weak than water, yet for attacking hard and strong things, nothing can surpass it. For there is no replacement for it. That the weak overcomes the strong, and the soft overcomes the hard, everyone in the world knows this, but none can practice it.

Therefore, the sage says: He who bears the reproach of the country is called the lord of the soil shrines. He who bears the misfortunes of the country becomes the king of the empire. True words seem paradoxical.

79

When a great hatred is reconciled, some hatred will surely remain. How can this be considered good?

Therefore, the sage keeps the left hand tally of the contract,[13] and does not exact claims on others. The man of virtue attends to the tally. The man without virtue attends to exaction. The way of heaven is impartial; it always sides with the good man.

80

Given a small country with few people. Let there be ten times or a hundred times the necessary tools, but they are not used. Let the people regard death seriously and not migrate far. Though they have boats and carriages, they would not ride them. Though they have armor and weapons, they would not display them.

Let the people return to using knotted cords.[14] Let them be satisfied with their food, pleased with their clothing, content with their homes, and happy in their customs. Though neighboring states are within sight, and the cocks crowing and dogs barking are within hearing, the people grow old and die without visiting each other.

81

True words are not pleasing. Pleasing words are not true. He who is good does not argue. He who argues is not good. He who knows is not learned. He who is learned does not know.

The sage does not hoard. The more he uses for others, the more he has. The more he gives to others, the more he possesses. The way of heaven is to benefit and not harm.

The way of the sage is to do his work and not strive.

Endnotes

[1] The first chapter is very important because it makes some very basic statements about the nature of the "way," tells how to observe it, and hints at the benefits of doing so. Sentences 1 and 2 say that a "way" that can be limited by describing or naming it is not the "way" Lao Tse is alluding to. His "way" is unlimited, impossible to define, describe or name. These qualities are necessary if it is to have the latitude necessary to "mother" existence. Sentence 3 says that this nameless, unlimited "way" is the starting point of the universe (heaven and earth). Sentence 4 tells us that the named (existence) is the source (mother) of all things. Although "the mother" means existence here, elsewhere in the *Tao Teh Ching* "the mother" refers to "the way" (the

nameless). The terms "the way," Nameless," "non-existence," "the uncarved block," and "no desires" are interchangeable in the *Tao Teh Ching*. Sentences 5 and 6 tell us that if we want to observe the secrets of the way, we must rid ourselves of desires; but we should keep our desires if we want to observe only the manifestations of the way. The "manifestations" are everything that exists. The "secrets" are the underlying meanings, principles, or causes "beneath" these manifestations. Desires are like mental attachments. If one is "attached" to a thing, he loses his perspective and objectivity. He will perceive the things in terms of how it relates to him, not how the thing relates to existence. His mind will not be free to "see" the secrets behind the manifestations. Strong attachments to a thing can result in one being unable to see anything but that thing: blindness of a sort. Sentence 7 says that the secrets and the manifestations are the same thing, but are named differently after they come into being. Some eyes see the thing, others see the meaning behind it (truth). So that is why, in Sentence 8, he says that because the secrets and the manifestations are the same thing, they are profound (deep). Profound and more profound. Very deep because all the secrets are before our "eyes" if we "look" right; "gateway to all mystery." So this is the nature of the "way" Lao Tse is writing about, and his method of observing it.

Many observations and conclusions are given in the remainder of the *Tao Teh Ching*. Note: The reader need not limit himself to this interpretation.

[2] Straw was tied together in the shape of a dog and used in Chinese religious ceremonies. The straw dog was treated with the utmost deference before the ceremony, but discarded, trampled, and burned after use.

[3] Man was said to have two souls: a soul of the body and a soul of the spirit.

[4] This probably refers to the belief that all living things begin life with a certain quantity of "life breath" or "vital force." This quantity is the source of their energy. Therefore, it is advisable for one to "breathe" (use) this limited quantity gently, like a baby breathes.

[5] Father and son, elder and younger brother, husband and wife.

[6] Etiquette required the use of one form of affirmation, or the other, depending on the circumstances.

[7] This may be a reference to the social predictability the Confucianists claimed would result from ethical culture.

[8] Perhaps "one" means existence, "two" refers to the yin and yang parts which in varying mixtures make up all things, and "three" represents heaven, earth, and man. All things are made by either heaven, earth or man.

[9] Pre-adults.

[10] The aged.

[11] Adults.

[12] The less it is handled, the better!

[13] Contracts were divided into left and right halves. The left half was the debtor's part.

[14] To aid the memory, instead of using writing.

www.ingramcontent.com/pod-product-compliance
Lightning Source LLC
LaVergne TN
LVHW041628070426
835507LV00008B/506